LOS ANGELES

miscellany

VOLUME 59

• • •

2011

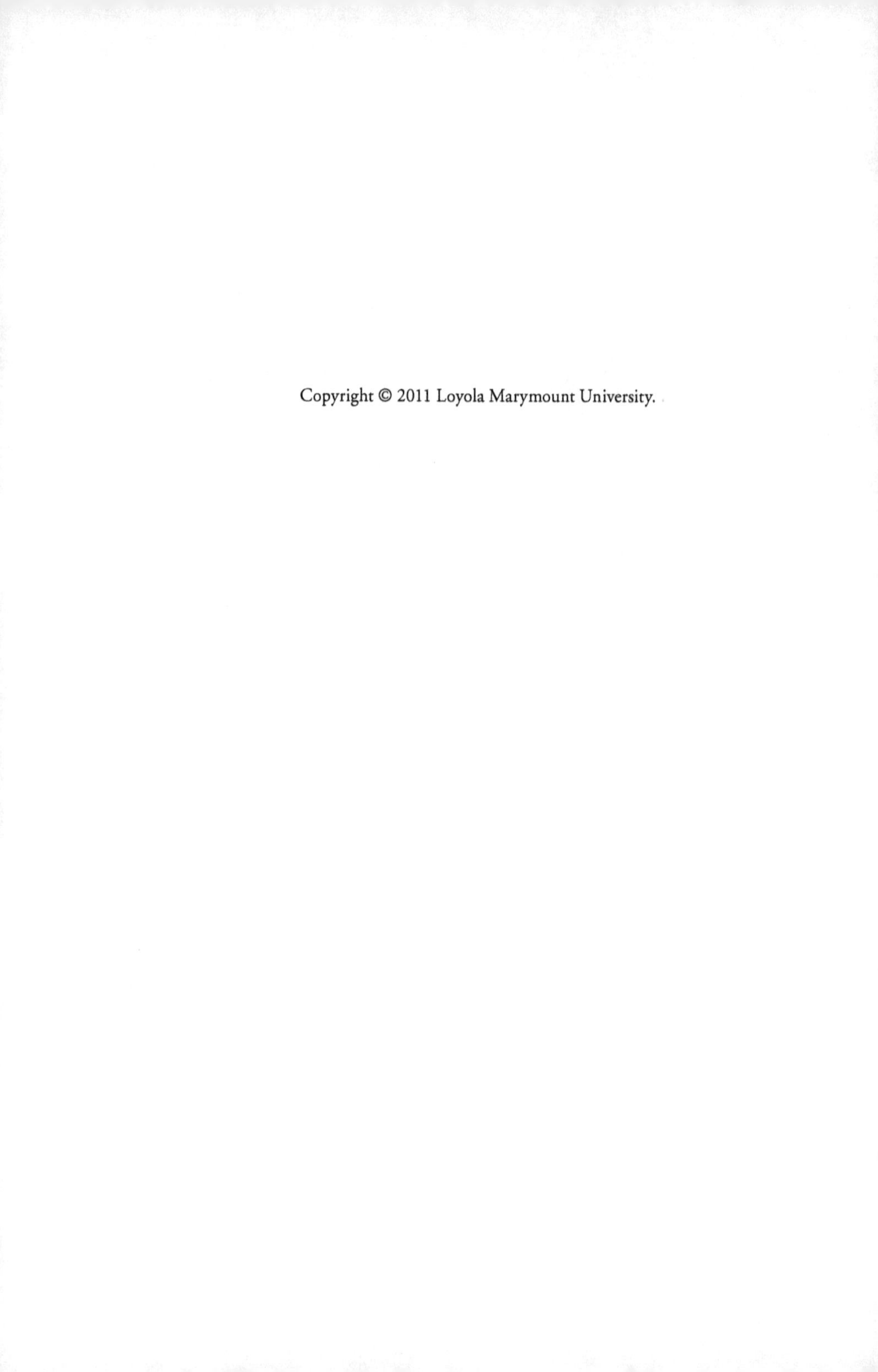

CONTENTS

BEAUTY IN THE EYES
Jennifer Pellerito..07

SANTA ANA WINDS
Leila Grace Pandy...08

FLARF
Spencer Daly...13

TITO
Robert Montenegro..20

TO ANYWHERE
Robert Montenegro..21

TAILS UP, LUCKY FREE
Grace Nowogrocki...22

ELIOT
Michael Broady..30

CRYING MAN
Raul Guererro...37

RUNNING INDIANS
Stanislaw Rupert Montovski...38

2100 STUNT ROAD
Louise Milligan...39

AN EYE
Ariana Quinonez...40

AFLAME
Kelsey Whited 41

MANUMISSION
Amanda Armer 42

A BOY CASTS HIS NET OUT TO SEA
Leila Grace Pandy 43

SKIRT
Mallory Massie 44

ELEGY/APOLOGIA/SERIES OF EVENTS
AND THOUGHTS OF THE HEARTLESS KILLER IN THE ACT
Raj Garewal 46

SEATTLE
Randall Templin 48

12 JANUARY
Mike Lee 51

LE SORELLE
Christian Pepe 53

MANIFESTO
Miscellany Staff 54

BEAUTY IN THE EYES

...

JENNIFER PELLERITO

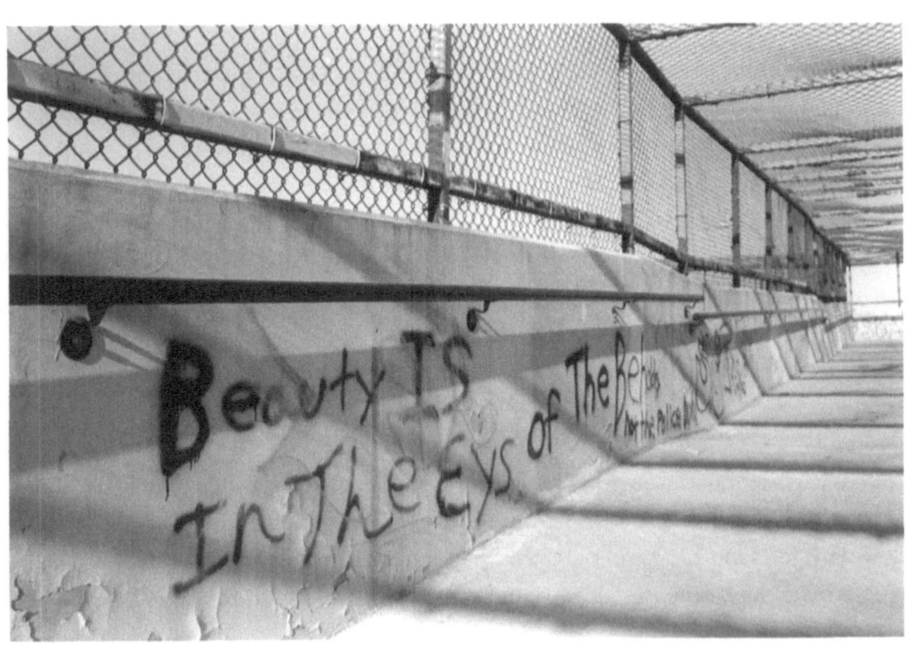

SANTA ANA WINDS

...

LEILA GRACE PANDY

You see a house sitting on the very end of the street near a lamp post with a soft orange glow—the light seeps into the kitchen where the window sits wide open and the curtains billow in the remnants of the Santa Ana winds—those curtains are of a faded blue gingham (mother picked them out because she knew the girlish quality did not align with father's taste for he was a man of cool greys and muddied cognac)—it is strange for the winds to be so strong this late in the year but it has been very odd lately, there has been a constant oddness in the air that cannot be seen or heard just felt—I felt it when the wind came through the window and into the kitchen and brushed against my shoulder, crawling and moaning—

The window moans my name: Mona, Mona, Moan—

Ah the kettle goes off twitching as the steam sputters out from the spout—the kettle is a tiny thing with rust crawling from the curves and corners—I had set the kettle down not too long ago and now the once quiet house sprung up with life—you are still hearing the kettle, it is all you can hear for it hisses and seethes—

You see me standing by the stove now, I hover over it and my hand rises up from my side and falls down on the stove's knob—it must be turned off—all of this hissing nonsense (why did I bother to make this tea, my stomach is not upset and I've already gone through the earl grey, and I've run out of honey—I should call grandmother—it is chilly in here), it must be the window blowing, brewing up a storm outside and the wood creeks under my feet when I fall back onto my seat by the counter—watch me count the chips—the grease coats my fingers—look, they glisten under the kitchen lights

The stove has been turned low—everything you see in the kitchen is in it's proper place—the spice rack is alphabetized, the placemats neat and straight, cereal boxes closed, candy bars stacked, but you turn and see the chips—they are scattered all over the counter—and you see that my hand hovers above them—my hand is shaking, my lips are dry, cracking—(something must be wrong, something is odd, what hour is it—the clock tells me it is late—what hour is it)—

The floorboards creek beneath my two feet—you see me stand up once again—I push the chair back—the legs screech against the cherry wood—the receipts from the supermarket and the drug store fly off the table—the wind grows fiercer outside—

There is a forest, a forest off in the far distance, beyond the swingset father built for the grandchildren—you stand in front of the kitchen sink, the steam wafting in and out of your vision—squint your eyes and you can see the forest, the roots and tree trunks creep up on to the trimmed grass at the edge of the property; the tree line is high, higher than it was when mother was a child

—look down, the clean dishes glisten back at you—I am by your side now and I am turning off the stove—finally the kettle settles and the clouds of steam disappear and the metal cools down—the air is stiff and still like bleached cotton and counter tops, toilet seats, paper table cloths—I wish I could bend forward and bend back, crossing over the assigned line that is stiff and still, unwavering even in the darkest of haze—

I will break out and run as far as these knobby knees will take me—but running is not appropriate, never in this house, in father's halls and mother's pantries—how I wish I could crawl up the walls—my mind is entrenched in this—

On the corner of this street, you can look to where the sun rises and see those beams stretch over the entire block—majestic lords—they create shadows behind cars, mailboxes, garden gnomes, housewives walking the family dog—footsteps fall into the pavement one after another—you can feel the street rumble when cars pull out of the driveway—pull back and focus—my house is still standing and I am still standing in the kitchen—

Father likes to tell me from time to time that my eyes look tired and says more protein more protein. A bite of chicken will do you a whole world of good (I thought a

cup of tea would do me a whole world of good, perhaps that is why I stayed up—no
tea no sleep no nothing)—sometimes father takes leftovers and dumps them on my
plate—he likes the color brown—tan, mahogany, coffee, russet—he likes the sim-
plicity of a knife— silver sharp edges straight to the point cut through dead center—
every so often he drops a piece of chicken breast on my plate and says I care for you
so please eat—This morning, you see mother walking down from the master upstairs
and you see her sit beside me at the counter—oh those Santa Ana winds—you hear
her say—I swear they kept me up almost the entire night with their hissing and
whistling—I tell your father to replace these windows, he blows me off—

Mother is right about that—father likes to toss her words over his shoulder—just
like that, her words go out the window—

Father quickly follows and heads straight to the fridge—you see the door swing open
and you can hear him shift through the contents before he settles on something
satisfactory—he turns to us—ah my beautiful ladies—a smile flashes on his face—
oh someone must've left the kettle on the stove—he does not move it off but rather
turns it on—morning tea

And that was morning and the day went by uneventfully and you see the occupants
of the house go in and out and finally when the sun goes down the shadows come
out—mother is standing by the stove now, and you see her stir a big pot of stew—it
is a rice porridge from the home country and it is hearty and hefty—the lines are ex-
panding—(Mona, one day you will learn how to make this, one day I will teach you
but first you must eat this, oh it reminds me of home, when my mother made it for
me when I was sick and I regained my strength every time—are you a strong person
with a strong will and a strong mind)

Sometimes I find myself crawling and gaping—my bottom lip dangles at the hor-
ror—the cavernous multitudes I just want to suffocate—(the smoke rises up from
the pot like a monster from the black void ready to eat me up and)—when dinner is
ready and then when dinner is done, mother and father are already gone and up the
stairs, leaving me to fend for myself

You see me by the kitchen sink once again and I hear my name once again—drown
it out—watch me drown it out—I turn the faucet on—water sputters out and when

it is too hot my hands start to sting and the steam rises above—a haze wafts into our face like a mist that crawls up from the loch onto the rolling hills and deep valleys— sweat appears on my brow

My stomach growls—you can hear it—the yearn vibrates in your ears and shakes the legs you stand upon—monsters lurk in the shadows (behind closed doors, on toilet seats, beneath nail polish) (mother has a habit of warning the duwende to move out of the way so she may have the oil properly thrown out) (it is for good luck)—

Midnight once again and here I am—you see me fastening the receipts from last week on the fridge with a magnet that mother and father got while vacationing in Vancouver—I can't stand this growling and this hissing—I just can't—you see me open the window and welcome in the Santa Ana winds—

The winds creep up and over the sill and howl past me, chilling my fingers to the bone—creeping over the kitchen counter where the granite shines grease-less and guilt-less—the wind howls, bemoaning my name over and over again—why must I hear my name—is it she that is trying to wrestle my attention away—sometimes I lose my focus when I grow thirsty so I try to make tea in the kettle from time to time just to have my mind settle down—she is a vicious monster and like the wind she flows into every room, up the walls, on the floor, hanging from the ceiling watching me with her eyes just as you watch me—

I would move if fear did not paralyze me—if I move I'm afraid I will open up the cabinets, pull paprika from the shelf and place it between cayenne and cloves (I like my toast with butter and blackberry jam, cereal dry—no milk please—I like these things a little too much sometimes)—when the wind moans she says something about how there is a fine line between me and air, clothes inhibit the hollowness of the void and she drags me by the hair howling and growling

The kettle goes off—when did I set that kettle down—the steam rushes out from the spout and the screeching is ringing in your ears and to me it is louder and it grows louder and it becomes this monster, a she-devil that cackles and groans—the kettle sputters out smoke—putter putter putt putt—mother and father are asleep—mother wants pretty dresses and kitten heels on my feet (father could care less)—you are seated at the counter and my back is facing you; you see that I am hunched over the sink—you can see my shoulder blades jut out as if they are gargoyle wings coming to life, breaking out from the stone, crawling out of the carver's hands—she is reaching towards me and I shiver—now by the kitchen stove you see me bring my hand to my face—a tight fist—I am choking for air, shadows grow, choking for air, the shadows grow on the floor— she is outside the window and I turn off the kettle—the curtains billow as the late autumn moon wanes into the night

FLARF

...

SPENCER VINCENT

Frank would never do anything to hurt the Jews because he was one. Well not really. His mother wasn't exactly Jewish—only his father and a couple third and second cousins. Also, he never practiced. So actually, he's not a Jew, but he said he was.

When I once asked him why he told people he was Jewish he said that first, because he suffers as a Jew, and second, that he looks like one. It's true. Curly hair, untamed beard, elongated nose, and a narrow face that would look unbalanced without his wide rimmed glasses. As for the suffering, Frank likes to constantly remind me of how his Grandfather, Stephen Glitzen, suffered through the Holocaust. Yes, his Grandfather suffered, but I remind him that during this time Stephen had a flourishing candle business that exempted him from the Ghettos, making him one of the few multi-millionaires to come out of the war. Frank likes to forget this because he says it hinders him from identifying himself as the starving, suffering poet.

 Frank and I never discussed age, but I knew Frank was 46, and that he sometimes wore a Yarmulke to cloak the halo of baldness at the top of his head. He would never admit that was why he wore a Yarmulke though. He would say that all poets are pious, and that a pious man has a right to wear a Yarmulke.

His Yarmulke was actually the reason we first met. 12 years ago, I was studying at UCI going for my masters in anthropology, and although I have always had an affinity for writing and words, this was the time in my life when I began to become frustrated with the construction and meaning of language. I was leaning towards a philosophy of essentialism, which basically states that everything only has an essence. Everything just is. Nothing more. And it makes no sense describing anything because you only take away from the "isness" of it. I enjoyed this philosophy, and I wrote plenty of articles for the school's creative journal on the subject, but I ran into a few problems with these essays as they contradicted the very movement of essentialism. I realized that I couldn't describe anything. So I began to write all my essays with just nothing. Just a period at the end of the page, as that was the only possible way to suitably explain my point. Below is an excerpt from one of my better essays:

.

The movement eventually, unfortunately, died because I couldn't get enough of a following from my fellow anthropology students, which lead me to abandon essentialism.

I then became a self-proclaimed realist, but I began to question myself. After watching hours of reality television, I began to first question reality, and then to throw it away all together. This was when I started Hypothetical Realism. In theory, Hypothetical Realism takes any situation that may happen and says that it did happen. Not much to it, but I didn't realize how murky the philosophy got until I began to practice it. I quickly realized that there was a fundamental problem with hypothetical realism. See the movement worked itself out in my head, hypothetically, but when I actually put it into practice I realized that the movement was no longer hypothetical. I was going against the very belief of the theory. I was in a pickle because you see, if I was to go back to realism in order to continue being a hypothetical realist, I wouldn't be a practicing hypothetical realist, but if I stayed a hypothetical realist, then I would be breaking the movement's one standard— that the movement be solely hypothetical.

This was a dilemma, and I decided to walk around downtown to find some sort of solace. This is where I saw Frank Glitz. He was wearing jeans, an old white T-shirt, and his Yarmulke. He was standing at a street corner watching a bum sleep on the sidewalk. I mistook Frank for a Rabbi; when I approached him, I got excited thinking that he might be able to give me the solace I was looking for. God could be the answer to my hypothetical realism.

I walked up to Frank and, without even an introduction, I asked him about God's actuality, His physical presence. Unsurprised, and without hesitation, Frank said that God's essence is what man can never come to yield to, while his presence is something inextricably to be misunderstood. I asked what that meant and he said he didn't know. They are just words. Then he asked me to get some coffee with him. I asked him if these were just "words," and he told me to stop being a smart ass.

At the diner Frank took me to, "The Dancing Khan," there was a surprisingly high amount of middle class white businessmen, and he told me that their clam chowder was fantastic. I didn't trust Frank at this point, so I got myself the Corn Tortilla soup with a side of blue chips. Frank told me about his mother. He said his mother wasn't Jewish but his father was. I asked why he kept referring to his parents in the past tense. He said it was because Jesus was his true father, and both his parents were dead. Before I had the time to feign sincerity, or even question his inconsistency of faith, Frank turned to the our waitress, whose face was as cold as a stone eroded by the ocean, and asked very kindly if he could have some more oyster crackers in his Clam Chowder. For some strange reason, Frank has some inexplicable craving for Oyster crackers.

In 1983 when Frank was 12, he would buy a lottery ticket every day in the hope that he could win the money and start his own chain of small diners in New York. He said that that is why he is so critical of every diner he visits. His diner would be, so he told me, a cross between a European karaoke and Jewish kosher bar. He says that this is the only thing that New York is missing. He hates New York though.

When Frank was 12 he bought a lottery ticket with the last number on the ticket technically a 9 (7-1-10-4-13-9) but misprinted to look like a 1 (7-1-10-4-13-1). This somewhat negligible mistake turned out to be a problem when the winning lotto number turned out to be 7-1-10-4-13-1. This somewhat negligible mistake turned out to be a problem when the winning lotto number turned out to be Frank's number with the last number 1. When Frank came forward to receive the 58 million dollar prize the officials were boggled, acknowledging, unofficially, that Frank had a right to think that he deserved the money. The lotto's board of trustees and directors were worried about a law suit and were prepared to offer half the pot to Frank until they saw that he was twelve. When Frank came into the office looking for his money, the lotto president Jimmy Jones, a man with no kids or grandkids of his own, gave Frank a juice box, a pat on the back, and a check for 1,000 dollars. Frank left the office and went straight to the deli "The Dancing Khan" and offered to buy the place for 1,000 dollars. The manager declined the offer, but he did offer Frank an exclusive lifetime supply of oyster crackers so long as he ate them in the Diner. Frank happily agreed.

Understanding why the waitress was so eager to satisfy Frank, Frank told me about his poetry. He told me he was a Jewish Flarfist. I asked if a Jewish Flarfist was different than a normal Flarfist. He said yes. He didn't elaborate. Then I asked what a Flarfist is and he said, Nothing. Then his eyes focused on mine and he pressed his folded hands to his lips. Everything.

I had no idea what he was trying to say, but I felt that if I looked contemplative and nodded my head a bit that he would continue his thought. He didn't. I asked if I could read his poetry, and he seized the journal on the table and said no. I asked why and he said, The Jews. This was another one of Frank's statements that I misunderstood both the content and context.

I left that deli thinking that Frank was either a confused Jew or not one at all. The next week I poured through sources looking for Flarfism. Surprisingly I came upon a few different recipes for a soft Jell-O pudding called "flarf." Open to all forms of art, I tried to make flarf, which I thought tasted pretty close to a strawberry banana Jell-O if it had been dipped in the toilet, but ended up only making limp Jell-O cones. After a few tries, I gave up.

The next few months I grew a beard, ate flarf, and searched any sources I could for Flarfism. It was surprisingly hard, and I didn't find anything for three months. The fourth month, I finally came across a publication called "The Brothers of Judas" which consisted of underground writings about the church, lighthearted movie reviews, and a medley of Jell-O pudding recipes.

I first realized that I had been making the Flarf pudding all wrong because I didn't let the mixture "sit" for 3-7 minutes before I put it in the fridge, then, after searching the magazine, I found an article written by Frank Glitz. He wrote an essay entitled "The Greatest F". In his essay he explained that Flarfism is when you take random chains of words and place them in a chaotic order within a loose structure of the poem. He argued that the subconscious would create meaning within the work and portray it though random word associations. He quoted one of his own poems to make his point.

"Children guns run crayon Babylon with twisted atoms bounce tiger lilies in hand of gold and wands of totems."

This poem was about Vietnam.

Frank was not always a Flarfist. He was first a deconstructionist, then a detrirealist, then a nonsensicalist, and now a Flarfist. He explains in a very eloquent passage of prose that he no longer cares for words, and he no longer finds power in the already constructed word associations.

Frank lived in fear due to his creative decisions. Ever since he was born he has associated himself with Judaism although he has renounced everything, cultural and religious, about it. Because of the strict hold that being Jewish had on Frank as a young man, he had to find a way to vent his "latent chaos" as he likes to call it. That is why Flarfism is beautiful to him. It lets him indulge in the chaos that church will not allow. This movement quickly made its way into the hearts of adolescent Jewish poets who began to Flarf themselves. It became so widespread that the church had to address the problem.

Flarfism, after some scriptural reference, was deemed as "unscriptural." Frank, of course, didn't think much of it until young Jewish men started arriving on his doorstep to learn from him. Frank took them in and he taught him what he knew. Considering that Flarfism was his own creation, he was just making things up each day and indoctrinating his students. Frank eventually had a group of about 22 staying in his living room; however, he talked about three that were closest to him. One was a girl named Ali. She was 23 and she was beautiful, but her poetry was even more beautiful. Frank quotes a poem of hers.

"Blazing toils reach falling stars binding hair and tortoise shells. Delightful."

Frank and Ali fell in Love.

The other two were two young boys. Frank assured us that he didn't fall in love with these young boys, but that they became his sons. These young men, who remain nameless and ageless, were Frank's closest friends and cohorts, and together the two young men went on to head the Toratics, a group of semi rebellious Jews modeled after the Haganah in the 1920's, which fights against Jewish injustice.

Little did Frank know that he was a primary enemy of the Jewish resistance. No one did, except the Jews. Frank began to become more taboo in the church. His works were censored, his character was defamed, and his name was placed on Zionist Synagogue's list of "unholies."

One morning, in the "habit" as his Flarfist students called it, Frank was teaching them about the importance of the word "thing." This was when they heard a hard knock on the door. Frank's two sons, as they came to be known, went to answer the door, and when they opened the door they were shoved against the wall and their hands were tied. Men dressed in black rushed into the room and threw in a smoke bomb. They created absolute chaos as they took as many students as they could, tore down posters, and hacked at the walls. Before they left, they threw all the books they could find in the center of the room and burned them. Just as quickly as they had entered, they left. Before they left the apparent leader (the only one that talked) told Frank to denounce Flarfism and dissociate himself with Judaism.

For many months, Frank did not write. He ran. He knew he was being hunted, chased by the Irgun, an extremist Jewish offense force whose job is to exterminate any threat to the Jew's freedom and well-being. He was frightened, but never so frightened as to denounce his Judaism. After 4 years of hiding in the basement of a run-down lamp store called "The Cave," he was finally found.

It was raining and Frank was skinny. He'd probably lost about 60 pounds since the "raid." He hadn't picked up a pen in years. This night, the rain was beating the rafters above him and he let his mind wander. He began to imagine poetry. He began to feel poetry. He knew he couldn't fight it anymore. As he reached for his bag, he heard three sharp knocks at the door and froze. He quietly shifted to the back of the room and covered himself in the torn blankets he pawned from an old Cuban man. He was trembling when three more knocks sounded. Frank could hear his own breath; his heartbeat jerked his entire skeletal body, as he could hear the murmurings of two men outside the door. Then it stopped. He held his breath then relaxed. A moment later, the door was blown open with homemade explosives, and two men dressed in black grabbed frank, put a mask on him, and threw him in a 2004 Toyota Sienna.

Nine years later, I was at the "Dancing Khan". I had gone to every week since I had met Frank, and ordered the Clam Chowder with Oyster Crackers. I had the same waitress as when I had first visited with Frank, and something odd happened. When she brought my Clam Chowder, she set it on the table, and instead of leaving, she leaned over and said, "Let me know how the Oyster Crackers are. If you need any more, don't worry about the cost. You can have all the crackers you'd like." She stood back up, smiled at me, and left; and at that moment I knew. I knew it was Frank.

TITO

...

ROBERT MONTENEGRO

For about seventeen years, Tito had a seat at the end of the bar next to the jukebox. He arrived before the vampires each day, before it got dark, coming from God knows where. He wore a Dick Dastardly handlebar mustache, painting him as a tie-your-niece-to-the-train-tracks character, but in a more tongue-in-cheek, vaudeville kind of way. The image was not ironic. Of itself, it just was.

The opening riot always took stage as the sun disappeared. The masks came off one by one, a dystopian orchestra of gnarls and skids storming in from the wet confusion of our imperfect atmosphere. The office lunatics had switched their ties for disguises, a masquerade of styles and fashions flooding in. The palm reader and the astrologer prepared to share a moment over Jack Daniels. Tito observed; a spy to their conversation, a stranger to their banal forms of contemplation, philosophical in the least and dependent on an opinion about a controversial Chinese diet. He tapped his foot to Tom Petty, a staple of his jukebox repertoire. Nickels clanged like cymbals in his shirt pocket, to the beat of life's performance.

Tito drowned a Pabst Blue Ribbon, a favorite of Frank Booth and a squadron of Echo Park hipsters. Fife the barkeep piously followed the script and granted him another as a stray torpedo reached the jukebox. The coin slot swallowed Thomas Jeffersons like bullets retreating back into the barrel of a gun. A hack melody rang true and the vampires danced as Tito drank and the curtain tumbled down.

Tito was dying. He had been dying every single day of his life.

... TO ANYWHERE

...

ROBERT MONTENEGRO

The small Mexican woman had come to pick a ticket, passage on a train to anywhere, wrapped in a shawl. Her shining green eyes pierced through the station like the light of a supernova. Bright. Lifeless. There was no future for those dying stars. Dust invaded and she shut them with a cringe.

She remembered the events of the past week. Her sisters had suffered terrible fates and she needed to escape. Esmeralda was kicked by a donkey and lay in bed, her mind incapable of clarity, her thoughts awash with the sterility of light gray and off-whites. Her sister Gloria was the victim of assault. The assailant, a complete mental collapse, robbed her blind of any sense of reason or feeling. It was the sight of her dearest elder sister as a vegetable that did it. It was too much. It had been too much even before this. Clara, the youngest, managed to choke on a grape, perhaps focusing all her attention on her unfortunate sisters and none whatsoever on her own unsteady mastication. Her funeral was Friday.

Now it was Monday, and a slender sugarcane body leaned on a pillar for support. With Clara gone, Gloria without her mind, and Esmeralda simply a shell of her former self, the woman was completely overwhelmed. She had nothing left in that place she used to call home. The night before she had dreamed of a white hunger, lean but rigid, meeting her on a train and promising her a red bicycle on a southern California ranch with oranges and grapefruit and six chickens. She awoke in a sweat, her hair still a mess, her dress stained with pea soup from the previous night's dinner, a meal she couldn't force into Gloria's mouth. The ghost of Clara was in the house, she knew, perhaps hiding behind a wall of concrete. She packed her bags and began walking. Clara would want her to escape. It did not matter where.

She needed liberation. The harbinger of freedom arrived at 2:43 p.m. that day in the form of an orange steam locomotive. It faced west.

TAILS-UP, LUCKY FREE

···

GRACE NOWOGROCKI

This is the kind of story you hate to tell. Not necessarily because it's a bad story (alright, it might get a little boring for some of you assholes) but mostly because you hate who you are in the story. Probably because you are still that person, aren't you? Maybe not. Only you don't know, even when you're finished telling the story, because that's the way these things work. Then you can't figure out what's more depressing, the fact that you haven't changed or the fact that you have. I'm kind of in that pickle right now. She says I should tell the story anyway for (what is the word she uses?) "cathartic" reasons. Nice vocabulary, that one. I'm not even sure this will cleanse my body mind soul like she thinks it will. I guess I'll just bore myself to tears. I might be biased. This could be quite effective. I guess it depends on the situation. These things are very situational, that much I do know. This story is about love. I know you probably just got blown over with the shock of it all.

It was my mother's wedding day. "My mother's getting married today." I said that to my reflection, like I was reminding myself. I'm not an idiot though, I didn't need reminding. I had this damn day marked on my calendar like it was Christmas or something. More like D-Day. Big red circle. Boom. Who makes their daughter the maid of honor anyway? I guess that's pretty standard. Maybe I'm the only person who finds the fact that my mother is walking down the aisle wearing a white dress towards a man while her 27 year old daughter waits for her a little odd. Call me crazy. The day of the wedding, I woke up without an alarm clock. She wanted me to help her get ready; it was basically my only duty beyond wearing a purple dress (that looked great on me) and smiling in all the pictures with her and Dave. Dave owns hardware stores (aptly named Dave's Hardware, what a fucking genius) and has a beard. It's grey. Excuse my French, but that's fucking ugly as hell. No one wants to look at a grey beard unless they're five and still believe in the Jolly Man up North.

My aunts were there to help my mother, too. They were squealing and they re-
minded me of my friends back in the city who I told not to come today because it's
embarrassing. They readily agreed. Maybe if they had any goddamn sense in their
doctorate educated brains they would know I needed them to come because I was
embarrassed. Christ. I thought to myself then, as I watched my mother drink cham-
pagne in the middle of the day, that maybe he would show up. Geoffrey. I never
called him that, but on my mother's wedding day, my thoughts called him Geoffrey.

Even when he did show up. Too far forward.

When I woke up on my mother's wedding day. Too far back.

I warned you this might be a bad one. I can't even get the order of events straight
and that's 101 type stuff, isn't it.

My mother drank champagne in the middle of the day and so did my aunts. So did
I, of course. It was a wedding after all. We were all manicured and waxed and my
aunt curled my hair. It looked fucking atrocious. Dave and I could be related with
our fucking atrocious hair. I thought I remembered something about curls falling in
the heat so I wanted to go outside. I told my mother I was going to have a cigarette.
She looked at me with eyes that said you know I hate when you do that because your
father did that and it turned his lungs to stone and they bruised his heart and he
died that way. Sometimes I wonder if he did it on purpose. Slow suicide is the grand-
est form of self-loathing I can think of. I think about that kind of thing more often
than most, that much I know. I smiled and laughed at my mother (can you see why I
hate myself here) and told her that I'm just going to have one.

Which is a lie, I guess. I didn't know how many I would have. I decided while I was
outside on the porch that I needed to get the hell out of there. It was over an hour
before the limo was coming to fetch (that's my mother's word) us for the ceremony.
My mother's house (I guess it's mine too) is quite large but it was feeling pretty
damn small that day. I hadn't been home in a long time. I thought I would go for a
walk. I had my cigarettes with me and my wallet too in case someone killed me in
broad daylight and they needed to identify my remains. If someone were to kill me it
would have to be for a really good reason. It couldn't be robbery gone wrong because
I don't have any money. None. Zero cash-fifty-bucks-in-my-checking-blew-through-

my-savings-years-ago, no money. That's pretty okay with me. Geoffrey liked to fight with me about my lack of fiscal responsibility. He has a pretty nice vocabulary, too. My walk really was supposed to be a stroll. I was just going to go a few times around the block, a few Parliament Lights, a few minutes before I returned to the land of tulle and lipstick and beading. That was the plan. My plans have a habit of changing themselves; I never change them. This is another one of those situational moments I mentioned earlier. You'll start to recognize them more now that I said it. That's how these things work.

My plan changed probably because I started thinking about Geoffrey. I started out thinking about my mother and Dave and my dress (my cleavage is simply divine) and then thoughts veered in Geoffrey's direction, that bastard. Of all our times together, I thought of one in particular. It was a morning, well most likely an afternoon (this was when I needed an alarm clock) and we were just waking up and he shifted closer to me and his stubble murmured on the skin of my neck like his whisper in my ear. He told me "you're beautiful." I didn't really need the compliment, I know that I'm beautiful and Geoffrey knew that I knew and he still complimented me all the time. Although, most of his compliments were like (I've come up with a pretty nice simile here) pennies on the sidewalk. They can be spotted anywhere but most are tails-up, lucky free. The few that you find with Lincoln's profile waiting for you are then precious and the luck you know they hold makes you feel protected (safe) for the day or a week or even longer.

I think I thought about this on my stroll (walk) because it was one of the very few times that I dared to look at his left forearm where the dark letters of my own handwriting were permanently tattooed. He had nice forearms; that wasn't the problem. I have nice handwriting, too. I practiced a lot when I was younger. I didn't really like to look at his left arm and that damn tattoo because of how he got it. The memory came with a replica of paralyzing fear that took me when I got the phone call about his accident. I ran in the pouring rain ten blocks to Jones Memorial Hospital, dripping on the white tile floors. I looked more like a patient that had escaped from the psych ward than a frantic lover, I guess. The nurse called me to the desk for information, phone numbers and insurance, but I didn't want him to wake thinking I hadn't been there; that would be lonely and it would really fucking suck to think you almost died and nobody fucking cared enough to show up because it was a monsoon outside or whatever. So I had to do something. I mean, I was in love with him. I still am most of the time. I took a pen from the clipboard (on TV they call it a chart) at the foot of his bed and drew a few circles on the carbon paper, to get the ink flowing. Then I wrote "I love you, I'm here" on his inner arm.

I don't know what he was thinking going around getting that tattooed there. When I wrote it his skin was so thin I thought the pen was going to pierce right through it and it would start spouting blood. I kept thinking about that while a man named Lord (yes, that was really his name, he showed me his driver's license) inked Geoffrey's arm later, blood shooting out and making a huge mess. They probably would have had to call the goddamn police or CDC or something. It didn't happen then, either. I think we would have been on television if it had. Geoffrey and I had a television experience once before, but there was no blood involved. I'm not really going to tell you what was involved because sometimes in stories there is a mystery and this is definitely, definitely one of them. Although it's not really all that mysterious, I guess. We could have been on TV if we had a cat that could skateboard or some bullshit like that. We never had a cat, though.

As I was strolling around my mother's neighborhood thinking about my (former) fiancé's lack of cat, I saw this house that was really familiar. Then I realized it was really familiar because I basically lived there when I was in high school. That doesn't really seem like a lot of time but I think you pack a whole bunch of stuff into those years and get a little carried away with the packing, if you know what I mean. I basically lived in this house with yellow (daisy not mustard) shutters because my best friend lived there. Her name is Anna. That's kind of an ordinary name, but it fit her well. That happens with people sometimes, their name just absolutely fits them. You couldn't pry that goddamn name off them if your life depended on it. So as I'm walking by this house that used to belong to Anna, the door opens and she just walks outside onto the porch. Like she knew I was going to be walking down the street smoking cigarettes and letting my fucking atrocious curls fall. She still lives in that small house with yellow shutters but when she walked out she was carrying a baby which I had never really seen her do before. She wasn't the type to get knocked up in high school, you know. She had a great reputation.

When she walked out onto the porch she didn't seem particularly shocked to see me around the neighborhood, as if this wasn't the first time I had been back to my house in about six years. She just waved me over to say hello. I went over and said hello and complimented her on her baby girl. You always have to compliment people on their babies, it's a rule. If you don't compliment them on their babies, what's the point in having one? I can't see a finite use for a child, at least not yet. One time I did, but that in itself is another story and this one isn't really going all that swimmingly so I probably should just quit while I'm ahead. She asked me what I was doing, wandering the streets and I couldn't really think of a good answer for that so I told her about my mother's wedding. Only she already knew about it because her husband is a carpenter or whatever so he works for Dave at Dave's Hardware (the man should win a prize for his naming ingenuity) so she was going to be there. She told me her dress was yellow (of course) and her babysitter was late. I was going to ask her what she was doing on the porch with her baby in the middle of the day but I didn't because I didn't really care about the answer. Sometimes I do that, just to make a point. Geoffrey says it is an irresponsible and immature form of communication because I guess he's an expert on that kind of stuff. Political Science majors think they're experts on everything, but they really aren't. Anna just kept blathering on about her baby so I stared at her and wondered if Geoffrey and I had gotten married if we would have a little girl by now. We'd probably be divorced.

When Anna finally stopped talking (I was wondering how we could have been such good friends) I noticed where the sun sat in the sky. I can do that you know, tell time using the sun. People think that it is a hard skill to acquire, but it really isn't. I mean I'm pretty sure someone could figure out how to do it without even experiencing some form of higher education. Maybe. I told Anna that I would see her at the wedding and walked back to my house. The only problem was that I still didn't want to go inside. My hair was looking much better though. I was glad. I wanted to look perfect in that glorious dress. Sometimes my mother really knows how to pick them. Sometimes. I was going to smoke another cigarette to avoid going inside but I decided that they may kill me so I should probably stop. I started breaking them in half, watching the deep brown flakes of tobacco spring out from their paper cage and just go nuts in the wind. That stuff really does smell good, I think that's part of the addiction. Or maybe I only think it smells good because I'm addicted to it. When I was breaking cigarettes in half, I wondered if Geoffrey's apartment still smelled like me. I thought about him an awful lot that day. I think it was because I was back in our hometown. Sometimes when you're in certain places, you think about the things that you don't normally let yourself think about. Situational.

That was when this great big white (ugh, how tacky) limo pulled into my driveway and my mother came outside screaming her head off about how I needed to put my dress on so we could all be fetched away. She didn't really say it like that but I think she should have for dramatic effect. I say things simply for dramatic effect sometimes like when I told Geoffrey that I had considered killing myself over him and he told me to stop being so maudlin (another winner word). I don't know where he came up with that stuff. I went into my old bedroom that I would like to say hadn't changed since the day I left it but sometimes I get into these very spontaneous moods where I tear down everything on the walls and burn it in a big metal trashcan in our drive-way. On that day my room was reflecting my senior year of college state of mind, and it had a poster version of Monet's Charing Cross Bridge and a framed copy of Hard Rain. I still like Bob and Claude, although my apartment in the city doesn't reflect this in such a disparagingly desperate way. My dress was all laid out on my neatly made bedspread (both my mother's doing) so I put it on and felt better because I knew I looked great. I don't know what the big deal was with this damn dress, but I think I was glad I could still feel good, even on my mother's wedding day.

This is the part where you're expecting me to tell you about the limo and the cer-emony and how it was beautiful and people cried or whatever. Well, you pretty much got the gist of it right there. Are any wedding ceremonies different? I should have asked my mother to make a pro/con list for me. I actually don't think she would have responded very well to that request. She can be cranky like that sometimes. We did have something that I think might constitute as a moment. Like one of those that happen on anniversary episodes of 7th Heaven or in Lifetime movies but with less talking. Right before I paraded down the aisle with my lilies (my mother's favorite) she kind of took my face in her hands. I thought she was going to give me one of those looks where I already know what's knocking around up there in her head but this time her eyes were saying too much and it made my heart dip and squeeze so I just asked her if she needed a valium or something (hate hate hate) and she said no, go get 'em tiger. Parting words, mother to daughter. I didn't feel quite so bad when I realized that I was angry because the situation was supposed to be reversed, remember?

The part of the ceremony that I deemed important had to do with me and not my mother (selfish) and it occurred right after I had my big debut as the girl who handed her the ring. I'm trying not to look at the rock already sitting on her finger because it looks just like mine (did). She basically went bananas over that thing and Dave noticed so he got her a similar setting so we could have matching rings. In some worlds, that may be construed as thoughtful or sensitive but I think it is pretty fucking creepy. Never, ever, would I want a ring similar to my mother's, just like Geoffrey would never own a business and name it after himself.

I handed her the platinum band and her eyes were all shiny and she smiled and I really hadn't seen her bust one of those out in a while. Her real smiles could knock you out sometimes. There are people who are always smiling, all the goddamn time, like they're Happy Meals with legs and you wonder if their cheek muscles hurt. That's a pretty viable excuse for not smiling, and I used it sometimes (only in certain photographic situations) and Geoffrey always knew I was lying and would make me smile later anyway, and that's all I wanted. I think sometimes I can be a little too predictable for my liking.

During the ceremony, when I was done with the passing of the ring, I looked out into the sizable crowd. I mean, it's not like everyone in the whole world wants to come watch this old lady marry this old man and have them making out all over the place. I thought it would be interesting to see who even shows up to one of these shindigs. Geoffrey showed up. He always knew how to do that stuff, how to show up when you told people you didn't want them there, because not everyone is a fucking genius you know. So he was there sitting in a pew wearing that green tie I bought him (could he be more in love with me?) and staring at a stained glass window like it was the most fascinating thing he had ever seen, until he caught me staring. Then he flipped me the bird and I blew him a kiss. I could predict the future from this moment. I knew what was going to happen at the reception and I didn't even want to stop it from happening. If I ever did have a super power like being a psychic, I would use it all wrong and only do what I wanted to do and not think about repercussions and certainly not about saving the city of Gotham or whatever. I know what you're thinking. It's not that, so get your mind out of the gutter.

I'm almost finished telling the story, just so you know. I hope you're not pulling your hair out with boredom yet. People do that sometimes and don't even try to hide it from you. It's rude. At my mother's wedding reception, I sat alone at the bridal party table so I decided to stand up. The only problem was, after I stood, I wasn't too sure what the hell I had stood up for in the first place so I felt a little retarded (I know that's not PC, get over it, it's how I felt) but I didn't want to sit back down. I didn't really have to though, because Geoffrey popped up (like he does). I just kind of looked in his eyes. They're not too special, just brown. But not that boring color where you can just tell the person is a total drip, but the kind that remind you of Hershey kisses and being pleasantly warm.

When he asked me if I wanted to dance, I just kind of bobbed my head like one of those toys they give you free at baseball games. Animate my face and put a bat in my hand and presto, I'm your free gift with purchase of one valid non-standing-room-only ticket. He swept me up into those arms of his and my breath went whoosh out my ears and nose and then I could speak again. This is what I was talking about earlier, in case you hadn't caught on. Geoffrey and I are really elegant dancers, everyone always said so. He swished me around the dance floor and we looked pretty great in our purple and green and everyone wondered why we weren't married. I mean, it's not like anyone shouted that out or anything, but you can always tell those kinds of things and I kind of started wondering it myself. Geoffrey decided to speak then.

"You know if we weren't so completely toxic for each other we would have been very happily married."

I guess he's a little bit psychic too. Maybe it's this goddamn town that makes us all mind reading mutants. Then I put my head on his shoulder (it fits perfectly) and pretended it was our wedding. I watched my mother step on Dave's feet and I saw another smile and since Geoffrey couldn't see my face, I let one slip too. Just one, before my mind remembered to forget.

ELIOT

•••

MICHAEL BROADY

After Al-Anon meetings Eliot was unusually relaxed, like someone on a train with a familiar book. He stood beside a foldout table with two pots of coffee and cups when Alan approached him. Alan held a paper cup in his massive hand, with fingers made for loosening stripped bolts. There was a tattoo above his elbow, faded blue and wrapped around his bicep like a tourniquet: "Bukowski." Without any prompting, Alan explained that he was a singularist; "someday," he said, "in the near future, our future, thoughts'll come, not from our grey brains, but from a cloud of knowledge up in the sky." Two members – Tina and Shane – walked by muttering, looking down at their feet and white linoleum. They discreetly explained to one another the end of…what? The tips of Eliot's fingers moistened against his own paper cup as he stood beside the foldout table. Bu – Kow – Ski looped over and over in his head. Bu – Kow – Ski, Bu – Kow – Ski, and then Tem – Pur – A, Tem – Pur – A. Alan's size was not threatening (he moved his weight with endearing docility), but some people can hold conversations comfortably with strangers; Eliot could not.

Walking to the parking lot, Alan gave Eliot a concise rundown of his recent routine: he woke up early, before ten, and went to a bar described by the German manager as a classic rathskeller. To most, it looked like a regular shit-hole. It was three blocks from where Alan stayed and opened at six in the morning. He watched reruns of classic baseball games while drinking Pabst beer. He complained about different batters' averages, most of them long retired. A few other men in the bar sat quietly in the corner booths. Eliot imagined them melting into the dark walls, becoming small knots in the wood paneling, forgotten and precious to nobody but the German manager. The manager's face, like a fathers, sagged under the weight of the dim light and dust, Semitic features framed by thinning hair and hanging neck skin. Then he saw the German with the face of his father or possibly his own aged face, waking up alone to massage his joints before six a.m.

The routine went on with Alan walking three blocks to his motel and taking a
six-pack of Pabst from his room fridge, to the pool. He'd write poetry by the pool,
although he said writing wasn't his priority. He did some drawing too. Often around
three, a woman he left unnamed, also staying at the motel, came out and sat by the
pool next to Alan; sometimes he'd follow her to her room or she'd follow him to his
and they'd spend the day in whomever's bed with the curtains drawn.

The two distinct images Alan stuck in Eliot's head, (1) his father, or Eliot himself,
aged and alone in a shit-hole bar; and (2) Alan sharing his days with an unnamed
woman, evoked something of an intense ache in Eliot taking the shape of fear of the
former and a yearning for the latter.

That night he dreamed he was in his own bed, watching an interview between a
man wearing a dark blue sport coat and an athlete discussing his team's perfor-
mance. When the baseball player tried to speak, his mouth opened too wide and
kept going, like a snake unhinging its jaw. Then his face was a big growing pool of
space, just a black void surrounded by lips. Eliot lay paralyzed, watching the bal-
looning mouth horrified, not of the mouth itself, but of nightmares he knew he'd get
when he closed his eyes. And when it was impossible not to give in to sleep, to hold
off the nightmares, Eliot closed his eyes and woke up.

A low three-legged table stood next to Eliot's queen sized bed. Cough drops, a
vanilla candle with a matchbook, a paperback anthology of short stories with a thin
silver lamp on top, sat on the table. A deep bookshelf on the wall at the foot of Eliot's
bed held the T.V. A collection of Steve McQueen DVDs was on one of the shelves.
Three posters with dark frames, none of which were made of real wood, hung on
the off-white walls; an old art nouveau advertisement for Belgium chocolate, the
façade of the Shakespeare and Company bookstore, and Manet's self-portrait. It took
some time for him to figure out the difference between his room and the room of his
nightmare. Eliot realized that in his nightmare there'd been someone sitting outside
his field of vision watching his reactions. It was early February.

The next time Eliot saw Alan it was June. Eliot had planned on seeing a Jim Jarmusch
movie fully expecting to leave understanding nothing. He parked several blocks away

from the theatre. Walking up the street, panting hard, Alan was looking back from where he'd come. With Eliot thinking of "Dead Man" and Alan looking over his hulking shoulder, they came close to collision. Alan seemed like a guy who forgot people quickly but they avoided impact and stopped to talk. He was tan, like he lived a little closer to the sun than everyone else. Eliot asked who he was running from and Alan looked over his shoulder again before saying he wasn't running from anyone.

By now Eliot was late for the movie and hadn't really wanted to go in the first place. Several years ago he got into an argument with a close friend who attacked his impatience for artists like Jim Jarmusch. He took it as a challenge and forced himself to see all of his films. To prove himself to himself, he once went to a show downtown dedicated to photography and other artwork inspired by Jarmusch films. A Latino man with a black suit led Eliot from an elevator, past canvases covered in the gloomy ebullitions of an obsessed architect in love, to an open room. He had shuffled from each piece to the next surrounded by other attendees who nodded or stared, taking part in some laconic conversation with the hanging artwork. The experience reminded Eliot of college business calculus; he was frustrated by titles with no apparent relationship to their accompanying paintings let alone Jim Jarmusch. One person (he/she had an androgynous name like Alex or Sasha but it could have just as easily been Taylor) painted an enormous canvas with assholes, free floating, and different birds from some fictitious-scape dominated by vermillion and yellow. Judging people's reactions, the piece—"Earth Metals and the Hush of Domination" – was tragic and ultimately powerful, but Eliot was far more engrossed by a painting of a woman titled "parent's spilt milk."

Alan asked if Eliot wanted to get tea and he agreed. He also agreed to drive Alan who said he had a load of lumber he was planning to use for a shelving unit crowding his car. Over tea, Alan invited Eliot on a boat trip with a group of people he had met through someone else at Al-Anon, which Eliot had quit. The following weekend the group of friends was going to take liberties and enact Bosch's Ship of Fools. They intended to send themselves off in a yacht and leave sanity anchored at shore. He didn't mention the Narrenschiff or Albrecht Dürer or even Brant.

Alan was enthusiastic about the event, lamenting the destructive force of reason, without which, we could enter into a truly shared creative state – it sounded to Eliot

like something not many people could actually think, or rather, believe; only maybe
certain bohemians and the deranged in which case the affair would be less of a
performance than it was presented as. It was an all night thing. He was aware of the
smallest granule of contempt for Alan and then there was an equally small fleck of
guilt for that contempt. And so Eliot didn't fully understand the concept, or neces-
sarily trust being out to sea with this man who opened himself up to strangers so
quickly, but he agreed to go.

On the boat that weekend people worked hard to embody their definitions of insan-
ity. The owner of the yacht, who acted out what Eliot assumed was some manic
disorder, brought cases of red and white wine. A man who he recognized from Al-
Anon clawed at the air while baring his teeth, apparently suffering from something
like lycanthropy. Wine was spilled and spit until Eliot could watch the boat rock by
studying rivulets of alcohol, Pacific in color, change direction. Over his fourth glass,
he caught Alan turning in place whispering to whoever passed him. It was a saturna-
lian event.

Much later, in the hours before sunrise, when the wine was gone and the frenetic ex-
citement too, Eliot saw something fragile about the way they danced into each other,
like the formation of universes or coalescing of previously burst planets, atomic
and important. Eliot sat apart and watched, alone. Alan was among two other men
and three women all sitting in a circle closed by their touching knees. They slapped
their palms on the deck and hummed. It went on for hours until people in the circle
started to lose definition, the way words can in their repetition. Everything collapsed
into one fine point. Eliot fell asleep listening to the sounds from the circle.

In Eliot's passenger seat driving home, Alan got on the topic of his next artistic
project. As he said, he was no poet. Not that there were any creative deficiencies in
him, but language was too ugly a medium. Alan hoped to recreate emotions and
memories by way of pulling sensual triggers. "I'll use psychoanalysis and certain
optical-neuro imaging technologies to get at memories and feelings, and uproot the
specific sounds or images or smells or tastes associated with each." Eliot asked for
more detail about these "technologies," but he only stared out the window. This
explanation was a movement in, a complex mantra expelled in long exhalations that
blasted Eliot's window in even, hot, breath. "Memories will be my new putty. I'll cre-

ate a set of different rooms that will become to everyone but the subject, a random jigsaw of stimuli. To one person though, it'll be a re-experience of past moments arranged whichever order I choose. Vestibule to the Ramified Self. Success means one individual can experience the exhibit in its entirety because it will be built for only that person."

If it worked, the implication was that Alan could reorganize people's pasts to create different narratives; he could start with newest and possibly future points to work backward, or loop adolescence, or even meld together different feelings to create heightened or discordant emotions. There was nothing so important, he explained, as this. Eliot let out a small laugh that sounded like a snicker. There was something supremely ugly in the sound, Eliot knew, and he had a vision of himself and Alan at the edge of some precipice. Alan was crawling to the edge while he ferociously beat at Alan's body until Alan threw himself from the cliff into nothingness. Eliot watched him fall and then realized the sensation of dropping would be gone eventually, leaving Alan weightless. He dropped Alan off at a corner near phone booths decorated in graffiti. At home, aching the same ache he had after first meeting Alan, he decided to sleep and then take care of things, knowing untended aches turn to bitterness.

Late in the afternoon he left his apartment, as anxious as he was thirsty, to drive through Los Angeles stopping at small bars he'd never been to with dilapidated signs and doors that didn't quite fit their frames. He drank only light beer until The Bridge. Inside the Bridge, Eliot approached a blonde woman sitting alone holding a glass of something golden. He introduced himself and she smiled at him without showing her teeth. She was drunk he thought. She was drunk but he was drunk, too. The bar smelled oddly of disinfectant. A man with jeans and a black tee shirt sat down at the table putting his arm around the woman. He told Eliot that Joan couldn't speak. "One night," the man said, "a couple years ago, we were at a place and a guy got too cozy with Joan. He had his hands on her hips and started kissing her," the man said. "So," the man said, "while they were doing their kissing I came up behind him and punched him below the ear." The man told Eliot that the guy bit down hard, right through Joan's tongue and swallowed it so that in her own way, she had been initiated into the Acephale. Eliot was upset. He stood up to walk towards the bar and the man and Joan began to laugh. She said something to his back that

Eliot didn't hear but it sounded like a command: read bad-tie and chest-off. At the bar he took two shots of tequila. From here on he only took shots, sometimes with, sometimes without lime. He moved from one dark bar to the next with a kind of melancholy determination, becoming heavily inebriated and losing self-awareness. At Town Tavern he passed out but only for a few minutes. He forgot ever going to Aces, The Sevens, and Luck's Tiki-Lounge.

Driving home, Eliot had the sick feeling that the palm tree lined streets he drove down were really overturned centipedes, each tree's fronds, helpless kicking legs. He remembered that centipedes are carnivorous and felt physically ill. Watching the fronds, Eliot didn't notice his tires driving over gravel. At the same time he chucked his belly full of drink, the left headlight and bumper slammed into the base of a signpost advertising a business park, shattering his windshield. With his head craned out of the window and his right arm reaching across his body to hold the wheel, Eliot's chest was nearly perpendicular to the steering column leaving the right side of his body most vulnerable. On impact, Eliot's right shoulder dislocated and his head whipped into the door.

In the following days he quickly associated the pang he felt before going out with the throbbing in his shoulder until the two pains were, to Eliot, the same. Only, sometimes it was more endogenous than acutely localized. He was told to wear a sling for at least one month after the accident and according to the doctor, would feel sporadic joint pain the rest of his life. The day after the accident, coming home from the hospital, Eliot found three different slips of paper in his pants pocket with phone numbers on them; two had names beside the numbers – Parker and Ella – and one only had the letter M. He didn't remember asking for anyone's number and could not guess at what the M stood for. At home he left the numbers on his bedside table and fell asleep. When he woke up he completely forgot the slips of paper. He walked around his apartment barefoot, inspecting his furniture, his fridge, his body in the bathroom mirror, with the distinct feeling that something was missing.

Before waking up he had dreamt of a childhood memory; he was running down a long dirt road towards home, towards safety from snapping dogs. Until his house wasn't his house, it was the house of a friend who Eliot could hear yelling behind him, but only when the wind slowed down and he stopped in the middle of the road to look up at the trees. They batted the wind and the sound of his friend's cries back and forth, swallowing the sounds and breathing them out. On his neck was a massive hand, heavy and soft like lead, guiding Eliot toward a marble staircase. But Eliot woke up unaware he had dreamt at all, as if the dream had never happened.

CRYING MAN

...

RAUL GUERRERO

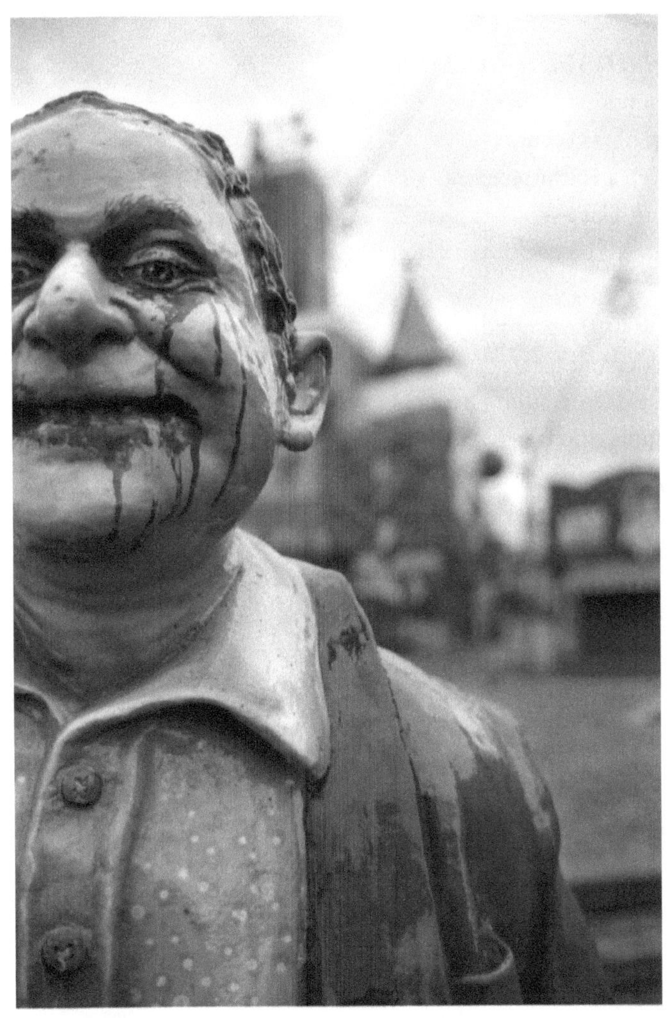

RUNNING INDIANS

...

STANISLAW RUPERT MONTOVSKI

Indians run with hatchets
from the mountains of New York
into the seats of taxi cabs,
and drive steep steps of progress
to spills of this place—
this place that all people can call home.

The moon twists the ground
Under knuckles and fists
And kicks the dust, cradling
Panicked haunts into wads of
Sequenced pre-planned events
Squawking in phrases that have no
Birth or death
          Be wary in sight of
The danger in God's sway and push
Somber tombs from holidays
And cake sweet words on sewage.

Three, two, five
          50 in all run away from redwood
sand into skyscrapers plastered with suits,
casted with manners.
          They put down their hatchets

2100 STUNT ROAD

•••

LOUISE MILLIGAN

The bare adobe bricks were unfinished.
I used to search for the occasional piece of straw,
embedded in the mud.
The house cried when it rained,
its tears would not fade for days,
when the California sun dried the stains from the walls.

Climbing through the dry creek bed out back,
I collected animal bones with my sister.
Some brittle from being forgotten in the sun,
Others so newly dead
We'd pet the hair between their antlers.

Tadpoles tested the speed of our pale hands.
We smelled like pond slime and algae.

We came home to a house full of bees.
They flew in though the chimney and died.
Every inch of the floor, covered.

We swept them out with the ash in the morning.

AN EYE

...

ARIANA QUINONEZ

Chocolate-covered cocoa bean,
take a spoon and
scoop it up. Opal stone
snowdrop dipped in the cup

and kaleidoscope saucers
twirling around flapping fans:
bristled brushes which
pan away the excess.

Hide the secret window,
the lights are on
though it seems dark inside;

treasured gifts lie behind
the door left ajar where
the waiting tiger sleeps.

AFLAME

...

KELSEY WHITED

Summer arrives as a fire,
swift and burning, an Indian summer in the middle
of a freezing winter, the frost still white in our hair.
Sweat beads on our backs, glides across our skin, slippery.
The bitter cold is no more as we move with the new season,
slow at first, then building rapidly as we learn to love again,
those beads of sweat across our skin,
in a burst of summer, unexpected.

MANUMISSION

...

AMANDA ARMER

We are cadenced though
We escaped from time

Ascended convention to honor
Free minds
Clasping euphoria
Dancing to fly

Vivid volition

Overwhelms the senses
Look, close your eyes, our souls are in bloom
Abandon monotony! Join in our ecstasy!
Air tastes ambrosial, just stick out your tongue

Or does this bewilder
And threaten in candor?
It must be hard to bottle up thunder

Elation, elevation—it seems—they're disturbing:
Grim steel forces now hover, obscenely,
To smother the fire we've stoked up quite sweetly

They think that we're dreaming
But we're truly seeing

"We dare you to stop us"

A BOY CASTS HIS NET OUT TO SEA

...

LEILA GRACE PANDY

A boy casts his net out to sea.
It bursts like a thick orange paint
That spills all over the blue canvas
Of rolling ocean waves.

A loud splash comes from above—
I see it drift down.
I want to swim away
But my fingers tangle with knots,
And my toes are caught in the gaps—
I struggle and feel a tug.
A force pulls me towards the surface.

Waves push me;
I can see his moist mouth glisten
In the sun; the heat caresses
My arched back...
The deep blue of my heart fades
Into air
And then
Into
Nothing.

SKIRT

•••

MALLORY MASSIE

She is standing on the corner of
Esmeralda and Tucumán
leaning against a newly built brick high-rise.
The fingers of one hand cradle a freshly lit cigarette;
the others wander and glide through the
pitch black waves that cascade and break at her waist.
She is beautiful; she can't be more than 18.
She has on a jacket for good reason:
it's freezing in Recoleta at 2am in late July.
But she also wears a short black skirt, her long thin legs exposed
even though it's not summer yet.
Mariana says that's how you can tell.
With one stiletto pressed to the brick, the other glued to cement,
she mumbles as men pass by, pursing her lips and
darting her dark brown eyes down
when she gets no response.
Something about the way she stands with her shoulders hitched up,
her constant hair fixing, her unnatural-looking cigarette puffs
tell me that she's no regular.
Santi notices me watching and nods to confirm:

Rookie, he says with a rolled R in his Porteño accent.
We, too, are outside leaning on a high-rise
and chain-smoking our Lucky Strikes.
I keep watching her, feeling like I am invading her life
but every time I look away my eyes come right back
to her there: across the street and slightly to the right.
Men keep passing, she keeps mumbling,
finishes one cigarette, lights up another.
A taxi drives up in front of her. He rolls down the window and calls out.
Her eyes widen a little and she sucks in her bottom lip
as she slowly approaches the car.
They talk for a minute. She nods her head. She doesn't smile.
She throws her cigarette, runs her hand through her hair once more, opens
the passenger door and gets in. He drives off.
I stomp out my cigarette and as I turn to go back inside
I catch one more glimpse of the taxi,
its brakes burning red to match the stoplight.
I don't see her silhouetted head in the passenger's side anymore.
She has gone, disappeared with the brake lights as
the taxi speeds away down Esmeralda.

ELEGY/APOLOGIA/SERIES OF EVENTS AND THOUGHTS OF THE HEARTLESS KILLER IN THE ACT

...

RAJ GAREWAL

Clint is dying. Clint was dying.
He lay in his big bed of activity and triumph, dry of all stains but his own. The bed he'd
built out of a breakup so he could have the appearance of a beautiful and adult life.
One that would attract another adult for life. One that would attract enough people so
that he would not realize he was stuck in Los Angeles,
Renting cars out, going to school, learning the finer points of Don Delillo's work so he
could get a job making money.

He dreamt about Alaska so his walls were white.
He lived low rent so his walls were thin and cracked.

It was never a convergence of misery,
not until recently.
We'd laugh the roil of the joyous
while casting lines into the lake of an anxious meth town,
never catching anything to fill our lives
which remained empty like the gap filled townie smiles,
though never were they stagnant.
There was a slow, inexorable downward roll
so gentle and slight, none of us felt it gather distance.

It was not the pull
of the dark matter empty gravity of our lives
that dragged us down and separate.

The delicate, surgical dismemberment of a pretty sociopath
was more than we could bear.
I tried dying.
Coincidence, nothing divine, ran through my veins.

Shaun bought pillows and comforters
thick enough to dull the sounds of sobbing
from Clint's room next door.
Clint cried the anguished screams of
the patient in operation without anesthetic
(Mollie is not an anesthesiologist,
nor is she a surgeon,
but she knows how to locate a diseased heart).

I gathered my coins.
I sit on pretty words,
stacking them taller and taller
to get away from destitute lakes
and asylum bedrooms.
I want to see the sky.
I'm making my way to heaven.

Clint is dying.
Shaun is dying.
I am ascending.

SEATTLE

...

RANDALL TEMPLIN

1.

Seattle made his way down
made his speech. There is a statue.
You can make almost anything
out of cedar. The statue is metal.
They baptized him and said he was
Noah. The rivers are named for his people.
The rivers and certain parts of the
sound and some of the smaller islands
the clamming fields that are private
property now. There are legal
disputes when the tribes break and
enter. They get tired of shaking
hands with Doc Maynard.

2.

The Melvins are playing the Croc
did you hear? It's a benefit for
a friend with cancer. All the old
head bangers are rifling through
their closets for forgotten flannel
and heading for Second and Blanchard.
Maybe they'll take their teenage
kids and show them the old haunts
Mama's and The Moore. They've
become software engineers since

Archers of Loaf had the grunge rug
pulled and Crooked Fingers turned out
better. Even Carissa's Wierd broke up
and Band of Horses made it
big. Let's prefer Grand Archives.
But Jurado and Bazan are still kicking
even when Jeff Suffering called
it quits. So that's something.

3.
Seattle could have slid down
the Cascades skipped across
the lake and skidded up to the sound
the way it spun to a sprawl splayed
flayed laid out in the trees surrounded
by mountains. A city with dark
streets under dark clouds nine months
a year both backs to the water with
trees everywhere. The hills make
the streets hard to drive but helped
the logs get down to the mill at
Lake Union in the 1880s.

4.
The hipsters are sledding down Denny
thinking more about cars than the

snow melting through their Converse
shoes certainly more than about
Denny. He donated the park where
they smoke American Spirits not far
from where Doc Maynard married him
to Louisa. There's an Indian on each
pack they smoke wearing a headdress
foreign to the cedar lodges that used
to dot these hills by the sound before
they shook hands with Doc and followed
Seattle to other parts to make room for
the logs and the sleds and the Crocodile
Cafe.

1 2   J A N U A R Y

...

M I K E   L E E

The most beautiful eyes she's ever seen she said,
from a stranger to a christmas dinner.
a paschal change,
spreading,
like the color of the stoplights on the pavement after the rain.

The rain rivulets around rocks and
gravel in the street
[s] of Paris
lines scaling the sky.

In that city, I see lines,
lines and lines and curves so long and so slight they too look like
lines,
and corners sinking into the overcast, cream sky.

Lines into gravel, streets into paths for feet.
rivers into logging rivers for bodies.
We wait for rice, we wait for tarps.

When the buildings fell, we were born.
Moun fèt pou mouri

We were born as buildings, a foundation.
Stones and mortar are our bones.

Rebuild with us.
Plane down my face, my shoulders, to straight lines.
Build us up to the sky.

LE SORELLE

...

CHRISTIAN PEPE

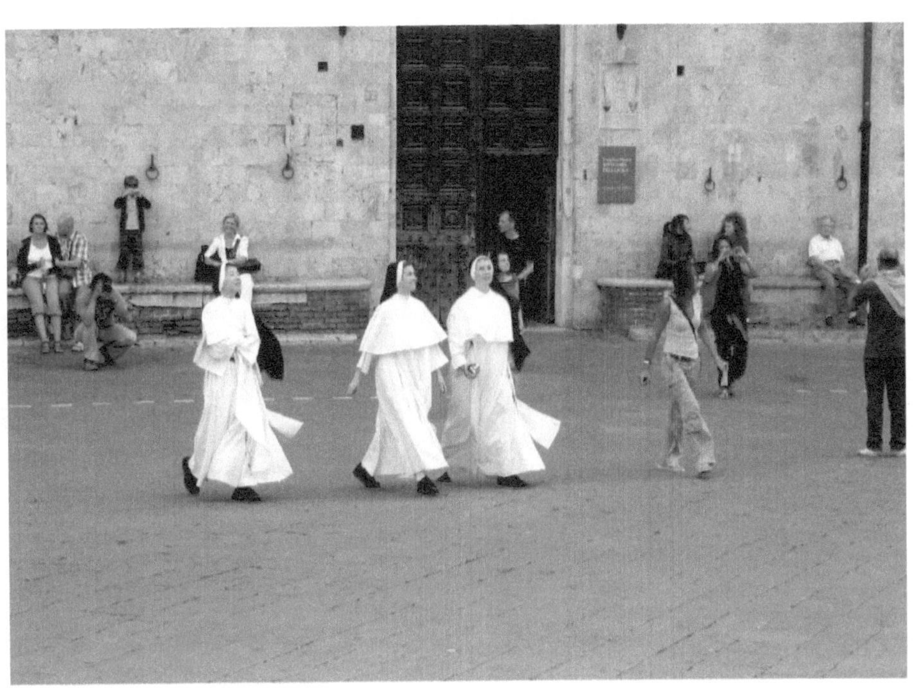

MANIFESTO

...

MISCELLANY STAFF

Manifesto
~~It's~~ mostly ~~beer. beer.~~   BEAR!

WE, THE AFOREMENTIONED EDITORS OF LA MISCELLANY,
~~notice~~ "beware of dogs" ~~notices~~ warnings. We ~~choose to
disagree. Please ignore that.~~   Please take notice
of the blatant grammatical errors   and the majestic ~~unicorns~~
up and coming writers of our generation. We stand to
acknowledge ~~greatness in our fellow peers~~ unicorns.
~~"They're all fucking avocados!"~~ I exclaimed with glee.
You can be sure we took   a page from
Hemingway + had a few drinks...
~~And then we asked "Who's Hemingway?"
and got into a... and ... and ...
we realized white people~~   All EDITORS
pressured each other equally and tequila suicides
were done by ALL editors.   —redact!
And we ~~kissed~~ and
the floor was wet, with ~~wet~~
the blood
of the decent cow slaughter.
And the ~~no~~ ink from the pen flooded
the page with the fluid insanity of
multiple shots — FOR FREE
In the hills of Brattleboro there's a chess
master who washes dishes — he's world ranked
He keeps his shoes in the oven and sleeps in
the hall.

→ ~~Recket~~!

[Mike Lee] is going to steal my Thom Yorke
~~story.~~ I told him (~~from~~ Thom Yorke) to write in
~~the~~ stream of conaiousness (If Thom Yorke ~~#~~ writes fiction
thank me). Mike ~~Lee~~ Lee ~~th~~ is stealing this story.
This ~~story~~ or experienced ~~helped~~ occurred on the
first atom for peace ~~at~~ concert (when they were
??? at the orpheum). Do not trust mike Lee.
This is Leila Grace. → ~~fiction~~
INTRODUCE NARRATIVE AUTHORITY!
and the language of diamonds
operates my tongue
~~LA RESISTANCE~~
        La Resistance
Flash Poetry. Nothing else matt
this is ~~the~~ future of the writte
word. TRUST ME

Mike ~~BROWBY~~;
? → HELP (. , mut)
word. the first several copies of the history
were ingested and caughed up as emoticons.
there were other copies which came out as
polished oak but too many termites for Moss Pro

Sp!?

IDK what is going on. an idgaf. the×lingo
is the new rethoric of the digital
generation. (It should) not be dismissed.
unicorns. —> cliche

Typhoid Mary lived on an
island in New York for transfering
Typhoid Fever to 33 people as
a cook. She was Irish.
It's legal, dammit!
She keeps mentioning unicorns...
they're mythical. Does that mean this
whole section is fiction. I'd believe
it. Drinking to writing... is this
acceptable?

It made me feel like falling
asleep...

SATAN, TURN UP THE DIAL!

Mike Lee IS TO HUMBLE FOR
HIS own good.
HER <— I am not sexist like hemingway

the most important
things are windows in
the prayer, making
ruins not about
a man inside who
flew he with fire
until another came
and spoke about
being built from
the ashes of a
pyre on another
ruin with no
father and no
history. In
the dawn the
man of ruin walked
from the home
and found a
truth
a town from
with ruins of mirrors

but ~~why~~ ~~did~~ you ~~come out to LA?~~ she
careful of mildew.
flip your latches

Lemon ~~~~ from a bum who turns bolts
like light bulbs
SMOKED   SALMON

Raj says and Kelsey says the same Mike wants to start
The world disappeared into itself
so we built a library to preserve
there were rows of books
of manuscripts
sometimes paintings
so we hid the library
amongst itself in its rows
of words   nothing.

unicorn?
alligator?

We know the literary world to be lacking. Poe
& prose cannot dictate the modern mouth, thus
we call for FLASH POETRY, a form which
can contain our thoughts & images in concise
forms, available to all.